D0842711

Conner's Big Hunt
by Shawn Meyer
Illustrated by Reed Sprunger

Text Copyright ©2005 Shawn Meyer   Illustrations Copyright ©2005 Reed Sprunger
ISBN 1-4196-0577-1

Third Printing 2007

All rights reserved. No part of this publication may be reproduced, stored in a retrieval system or transmitted in any form by any means, electronic, mechanical, photocopy, recording or otherwise, without the prior permission of the publisher, except as provided by USA copyright law.

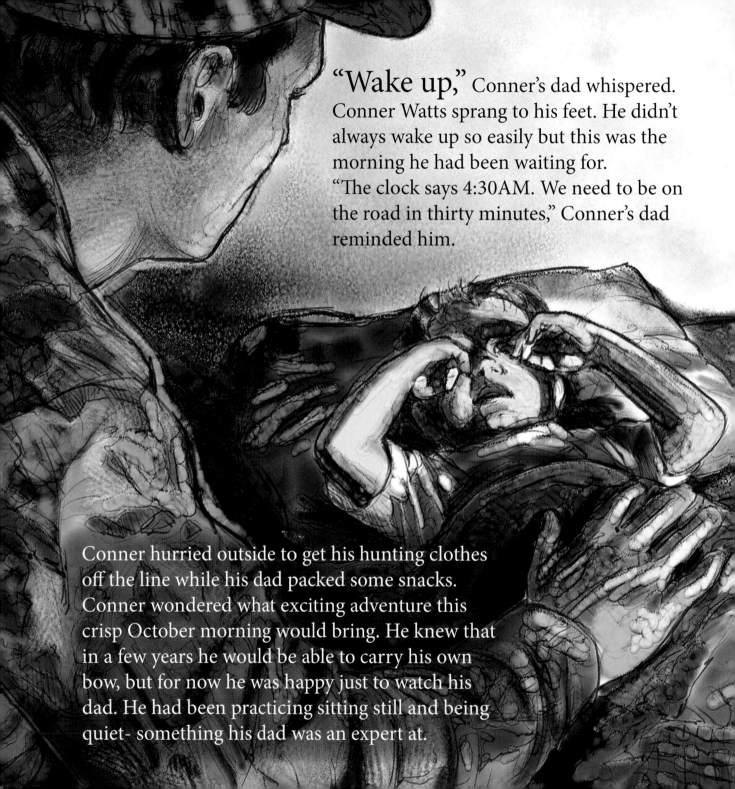

"Wake up," Conner's dad whispered. Conner Watts sprang to his feet. He didn't always wake up so easily but this was the morning he had been waiting for.

"The clock says 4:30AM. We need to be on the road in thirty minutes," Conner's dad reminded him.

Conner hurried outside to get his hunting clothes off the line while his dad packed some snacks. Conner wondered what exciting adventure this crisp October morning would bring. He knew that in a few years he would be able to carry his own bow, but for now he was happy just to watch his dad. He had been practicing sitting still and being quiet- something his dad was an expert at.

Conner's dad quizzed him
while they got ready.
"Do you have your binoculars Conner?"
    "Yes, Dad."
"What about your knife?"
    "Got that too, Dad."
"Looks like we're ready."

The drive to Mrs. Cole's
farm took fifteen minutes but to
Conner it seemed more like an hour.
When they arrived, Mr. Watts parked the
truck on top of the hill.
"Remember, no more talking once we cross the
fence unless it's really important."
        "Okay, Dad."
As Conner and his dad reached the fence they
noticed that a big tree limb had fallen on it. That
made crossing it easier than usual.

Conner wasn't afraid of walking in the dark when he was with his dad. The worst part was going through the wet grass. Even Conner's tall boots couldn't keep the dew from soaking his legs.

Soon Conner and his dad reached the treestand.
The first thing to do in a treestand is put on your safety harness.
When they were safely tied in, Mr. Watts pulled up his bow.
Then he looked at his watch.
Very softly he whispered to Conner, "Twenty minutes before
legal shooting time. For now, just relax and listen to the sounds."

At first there weren't any sounds to listen to. But soon the woods came alive. Even though it was still dark, Conner could tell that most of the sounds were birds.

Conner couldn't wait for it to get light. Suddenly something walked directly underneath them. Conner turned quickly to follow the sound of crunching leaves and snapping twigs. Then he felt his dad's hand on his arm. He knew that was a reminder to sit still.

It finally started
to get light.
Conner's dad nocked his
arrow. The hunt was on.
Conner remembered his dad's
advice, "If you have to move,
move as slowly as you can. Then,
when you think you can't move
any slower, slow down."

Conner detected motion. A deer! He started to turn to tell his dad but he felt the familiar squeeze on his arm that told him dad already saw the deer.
It was a doe. Soon, two yearlings approached. Yearlings are deer that haven't grown up. They usually stay close to their mothers.

Conner enjoyed watching the doe and her yearlings. Conner's dad had told him that it's a good morning when you see deer and it's a great morning if they don't see you. It was already a great morning! It wasn't long till the three deer meandered away and out of sight.

All was still again except for a very busy fox squirrel. Conner wondered if he'd ever get to see his dad shoot a deer. Mr. Watts was waiting for a buck. Conner had never seen a buck unless you count ones that were already dead. But his luck was about to change.

His eyes were starting to get sleepy when Conner felt the squeeze again. This time he knew to sit still. Something was about to happen.

The faint sound of steps came from his left. In the corner of his eye, Conner saw a deer pacing closer.

Soon
he could see
a magnificent set
of antlers. Conner's
heart pounded with
excitement! Mr. Watts
drew his bow.

The buck stopped.
Conner wondered why his
dad was not shooting but he
knew he couldn't ask.
The deer reached back and
licked its side then started
moving again, following the
path. Conner couldn't believe it:
His dad was going to let the big
buck walk away.
The grunting noise startled Conner.
It was his dad's way of telling the buck
to stop for a second. And it worked!
The buck looked back.

Everything happened
really fast after that. No sooner did
Conner hear the arrow release than
he watched the buck disappear into
the distance.
It felt like the greatest moment of Conner's
life. Conner's dad leaned over and said,
"It was a good hit. We should have no
trouble finding him."
After that he looked
at his watch.

Thirty minutes of waiting seemed like forever to Conner. When the time was up, Conner and his dad followed a steady blood trail right to the deer.

"Ten points! How about a picture?"

"Yeah!" Conner shouted as he struggled to raise the buck's head.

Conner got to carry the bow
on the way back as his dad dragged the big
buck up to the fence.
"We'll leave him here and get the truck,"
Conner's dad said.

They returned with the truck
and loaded the heavy deer into the bed.
"We just have one more thing to do."
        "What's that?" Conner asked.
"Fix the fence."
At first Conner didn't want to take time out of their
exciting morning to fix a fence, but he'd soon understand.
Mr. Watts wrestled the dead maple limb off the fence.
Then he took some tools out of his
truck and repaired the
damage. "Now,
let's go show
this buck to
Mrs. Cole.
She'll be
excited!"

Mrs. Cole was working in the yard when she saw the truck pull around the barn. "Either you fellows got a deer or you give up easily," she said as she made her way to the truck.

"Mrs. Cole, Conner and I want to thank you very much for the privilege of hunting here." "You are very welcome," Mrs. Cole replied as she admired the buck, "You and Conner may come back anytime, especially if you plan to share some of those venison steaks."

"It's a deal!" replied Conner.

Conner couldn't wait to get home and show the buck to his mom. "Dad, we didn't tell Mrs. Cole that we fixed her fence," Conner announced. "The reason we fixed the fence is because helping out is the right thing to do, Conner. Let's just keep it our little secret, okay?" Conner nodded.

"Conner, I'm sure glad you came along this morning. For years to come we'll both think back to this hunt. Every time you do, I'd like you to remember the lesson you learned about the importance of helping."

"I will, Dad," Conner said with a smile.

A note to parents:

In recent years it has become increasingly clear to us that the future of hunting, fishing, and trapping is in the hands of our children. In response to this awareness, many fine programs have been developed for the purpose of generating interest and encouraging ethics among children. And thankfully so.

As useful as such programs are, and as much as we all ought to support them, they will never replace the role of parents. You are still the greatest influence in your child's life. That's the way it should be. If the future of hunting is in the hands of our children then our children are in *our* hands.

But it's about more than simply protecting our traditions. It's about acknowledging what is most important in life. The great outdoors offer the perfect context for sharing magical moments. When their eyes light up with excitement, we know that we have just made a lasting memory.

So, it's about ethics. It's about character building. It's about preserving our priceless traditions. And it's about relationships and enduring memories.

It has been said that no one looks back at the end of life and laments, "I just wish I'd have spent more time at work." I would add that no hunter will say, "I just wish I would have left my child at home and gone hunting alone that day."

So make sure your "take along" list includes a kid. And good luck!

For more information visit www.huntwithakid.com
While reading this book, see if you can find the hidden creature(s) in each outdoor scene.